# POEMS IN THE KEYS OF LIFE

Henry Lee Thomas

Poems in the Keys of Life by Henry Lee Thomas

Copyright © 2019 by Henry Lee Thomas.

All rights reserved. No part of this book may be reproduced in any form or by any electronic or mechanical means including information storage and retrieval systems without permission in writing from the author except in the case of brief quotations included in critical articles and reviews. For information, please contact the author.

Cover Design: Henry Lee Thomas and maxphotomaster
Cover Art: Stock Photo Secrets
Other Photos/Illustrations: Stock Photo Secrets
Editing: Evy Zen

Printed & bound in the United States of America

First Edition

www.PoemsInTheKeysOfLife.com
hthomas@notjustformen.com

Library of Congress Control Number: 2018914349

ISBN-13: 978-1-970144-00-0 (Paperback Edition)
ISBN-13: 978-1-970144-01-7 (Hardcover Edition)

POETRY / Subjects & Themes / General

# Dedication

In honor of my parents, Henry Jr and Pauline, who gave me everything I needed to succeed. The rest was on me.

Also to the strength and support I received over the years from my siblings Alma, Patricia, Larry, Hattie, Cassandra, and Jerome.

Finally, to my son Henry Ethan, hoping that he will learn the difference between friend & foe; and that life is a marathon, not a sprint.

# Legal Statement

This book is a work of fiction. Names, characters, and incidents either are products of the author's imagination or are used fictitiously. Any resemblance to actual events or persons, living or dead, is entirely coincidental.

# Contents

**INTRODUCTION** ................................................................ 1
**LIFE IS LOVE** .................................................................. 3

**I: KEY OF BIRTH** ............................................................. 5
    Birth ............................................................................. 7
    A Child Is Born ........................................................... 8
    New Birth ..................................................................... 9
    New Life ..................................................................... 10
    Seed ............................................................................ 11
    Test Tube Baby ......................................................... 12

**II: KEY OF CHILDHOOD, SCHOOL, & WORK** ............ 13
    Little Feet .................................................................. 15
    I See Big People ........................................................ 16
    Grading Papers ......................................................... 17
    Homework .................................................................. 18
    The Mighty Green Waves ....................................... 19
    Junkyard .................................................................... 20
    Liberal Arts ............................................................... 21

**III: KEY OF LOVE, SEX, & MARRIAGE** ....................... 23
    Ode to Love ............................................................... 25
    Sexes in Harmony .................................................... 26

| | |
|---|---|
| Soul Mates | 27 |
| Circle of Love | 28 |
| Convergence | 29 |
| Living with the Enemy | 30 |
| Deep in the Well | 31 |
| Venom | 32 |
| Touch Me Here | 33 |
| Love – Where is it? | 34 |
| Love is Not a Passing Star | 36 |
| Transitions | 37 |
| Love Is Not Enough | 38 |
| Love Analyzed | 39 |
| Falling | 40 |
| Fall | 41 |
| Alley Walking | 42 |
| Newness | 43 |
| Love Transformed | 44 |
| Amoura | 45 |
| Cherries | 46 |
| Don't Tread On Me | 47 |
| Truth Be Told | 48 |
| Straight from the Heart | 49 |
| Kiss | 50 |
| Living La Vida Amorosa | 51 |
| Deep Love | 52 |

Heat ..................................................................... 54
Pleasure ............................................................... 55
Marriage .............................................................. 56

## IV: KEY OF FAMILY .................................................. 57

Family .................................................................. 59
Bad Behavior ...................................................... 60
A Family Affair .................................................. 61
Why Did You Poison Our Son? ......................... 62
Raising Children ................................................ 66
Family Tree ........................................................ 67
Siblings ............................................................... 68
You Can Always Go Back Home ...................... 69

## V: KEY OF INTERACTION WITH NATURE ........ 71

Weeds .................................................................. 73
Spring .................................................................. 74
Phases ................................................................. 75
The Wind ............................................................ 76
Ocean Waves ...................................................... 77
Black Bird ........................................................... 78

## VI: KEY OF MIND STREAMS ............................... 79

Knowledge .......................................................... 81
Questions ............................................................ 82

Popsicle Stick ............ 83

Black and White ............ 84

Trading Places ............ 86

Way ............ 87

Bias in Our Midst ............ 88

Energize ............ 89

Coming Out ............ 90

Majority ............ 91

Tommie Smith ............ 92

Waves ............ 94

Lost ............ 95

Wanderer ............ 96

The God within Us ............ 97

VII: KEY OF RETIREMENT & DEATH ............ 99

Retirement ............ 101

Joy Delayed ............ 102

Closed Door ............ 103

Black Hole ............ 104

Mourning ............ 105

REBIRTH ............ 107

ABOUT THE AUTHOR ............ 109

~ x ~

# INTRODUCTION

In music, a key is a family of notes and chords which are derived from the Chromatic Scale. There are 12 major keys and 12 minor keys in music theory. Music in different keys provokes a different "feel" or emotion from the listener. Another way to look at it is, in general, all songs within the same key have a distinct favor or character to them which is perceived by the listener. In addition, there are 7 letters used in the musical alphabet (A through G) to define keys. These keys are used to produce beautiful melodic music.

Poems can have a musical melody of their own. Just as you can enjoy the lovely vocal melodies in music such as Verdi's "Rigoletto", poems can achieve the same level of beauty. After all, many songs are created from poems!

In life I define a key as "the major events/emotions/thoughts which dominate a person's life". These life events can elicit the same emotions (both positive and negative) as music can. You can also think of it as stressful events. Of course, stress can be both positive and negative. I believe that life, poetry, and music are closely intertwined. There is a synchronicity between them which cannot be denied.

Thus, I am grouping my collection of poems into 7 sections to play off of the number of letters used in the musical lexicon. These sections roughly represent the major states, emotions, and thoughts (Keys) in life:

Major Keys of Life

1. Birth
2. Childhood, School, & Work
3. Love, Sex, & Marriage
4. Family
5. Interaction with Nature
6. Mind Streams
7. Retirement & Death

This organization represents my mind map which shows that poetry impacts us at every stage and state of our lives.

The association of musical keys with major events, emotions, and thoughts is well understood by students and lovers of music. Think of the emotions which are released when people sing their country's national anthem, when you listen to Mozart's Lacrimosa (from Requiem), Diana Ross and Lionel Richie's 'Endless Love', or 'Hush Little Baby' to name a few. All these songs within each of their categories elicit a common emotion, a common 'tonic'. That is, the songs within a key have a unique relationship with each other which is different than songs in another key. The same holds true for poems.

When you listen to a poem about birth, for example, your emotional response will be significantly different than when you listen to a poem about death. Though there is probably somewhat of an overlap (as is the case with musical keys), the poems in each of my 'keys' will have a similar emotional impact when you read them.

As you read my compositions, allow yourself to feel the emotion and enjoy the music!

# LIFE IS LOVE

# I: KEY OF BIRTH

# Birth

Birth is a natural, biological, organic process:
An interaction combining two into one,
A part of you and a part of me,
A random subset of DNA.
Who will evolve?
Let's wait.
Let's see.

## A Child Is Born

Love is in the air.

I sense explosions and heat.

A new child is born.

# New Birth

Rumblings within,
A buildup of tension,
Divisions across the pond,
How much more can we take?
We won't.
Let's go.
Where to?
A new birth, a new nation.

# New Life

New life in my belly.
How will this change our life?
Will he make time to help?
What about us?
Can we?
Can he?
What about me?

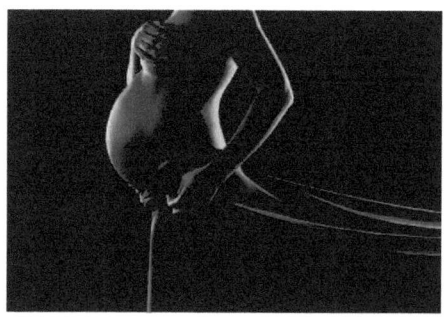

## Seed

From a seed comes life.
Give it water and feed it,
So it can mature and prosper.
Protect it from that which harms it.

It can also be a thought,
A suggestion,
A desire.
Plant it and see what happens.

## Test Tube Baby

We did not meet in the usual way.
We met in a petri dish.
Not properly introduced
But expected to come together.

We circled the dish,
Getting to know each other,
Checking each other out,
Deciding whether to mix.

As time passed,
I began to warm to your advances
And allowed myself
To be entered.

# II: KEY OF CHILDHOOD, SCHOOL, & WORK

## Little Feet

Little feet in my garden,
Running fast and free.
Watch out for that tree!

Laughing and giggling with glee.
Oh no, I have to pee!
Time to let it free!

## I See Big People

As I celebrate my second birthday—
Or is it my third?
All I see is big people,
Towering above me like Georgia pines,
Not taking me seriously,
Using words I don't understand.

Yea, they feed me and stuff,
But how do I navigate this world,
Find my own place in it,
When I don't know how?

I can only hope
That one day I will be big too,
So I can feel safer.

## Grading Papers

Digging through test papers...
How many students are there?
Stained and crumbled pages...
Does anyone care?
Low pay...
Where's the aspirin?

## Homework

Just when
You thought
It was safe
To go home,
You had to
Help your kid
With homework!
Maybe I should reconsider?

## The Mighty Green Waves

I realized the power of school spirit
During my senior year
At Spencer High School:
The Green and Gold,
The Owls,
The Green Waves.

It was the end of segregation,
When schools in the city were being
integrated.
A test of our mettle,
To change our glorious history,
To merge divergent factions,
Into a united whole.

We entered that year
With great anticipation,
Hoping to achieve
A new Green Wave nation.

It was a testament to my classmates
That we were able to consolidate,
To become one integrated team.

For this I commemorate
Our ability to band together,
To achieve a new school spirit.
Long live the Mighty *New* Green Waves!

# Junkyard

My father worked in a junkyard:
Old cars, tires, batteries, and trucks;
The smell of oil, gas, and dust;
The howling of the junkyard dog;
Pulling parts and other stuff;
Hard work and low pay;
Deals to be had
By the poor and thrifty.

That's where I got my first car.
You do what you have to do
To make a living,
To raise a family—
Even if it's in the junkyard.

## Liberal Arts

Going to college for Liberal Arts,
Don't really know what it is...
Liberal Arts, LA, sounds like one of those California degrees
Or something invented by those damn Yankees.

They say it will make me a Jack of all Trades,
A Renaissance man.
It really means I don't know what I want to do in life.

Maybe it allows me to buy some time,
To delay my ascent into adulthood.
And when I finish I can work in one of those Trades I learned.

And if that doesn't work out, I can be a Liberal Arts teacher.
I hear they are hiring.

# III: KEY OF LOVE, SEX, & MARRIAGE

## Ode to Love

Oh what sweet tasting honey we do seek,

Dripping all over our bodies complete.

Thoughts of caressing & kissing our cheeks,

While making love under the silky sheets.

Let us agree to continue to meet

In love's embrace as we drift off to sleep.

## Sexes in Harmony

Men and women here,
Born to do things differently,
Still in harmony.

## Soul Mates

So you think you are soul mates?
Obviously that can't be true.
Understand that there is no such thing.
Love is fleeting.
Maybe it will last.
All things considered,
Two can be better than one.
Ease up though—
Search your soul to find the answer.

## Circle of Love

Our love is not angular.
It's smooth and flowing.
It radiates outward and inward.
We are equal distance from our center.

As we rotate, we stay in sync.
We allow others in
Without perturbations.
When we go in opposite directions,
We always come back together again.

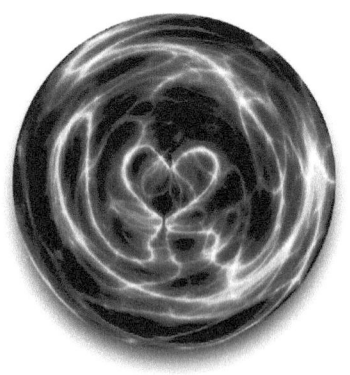

## Convergence

Two beings drifting in the sea of life,
Evolving in similar ways under
Different conditions.

Sense the pull of attraction, the urgency
To feel, to touch, to embrace.

We get us,
As we move towards a union of one.

## Living with the Enemy

Be careful who you bed with.
Looks can be deceiving.
Look for the underbelly.
It's there that you can seek the truth.
You were looking for a soulmate, not a mole.

No one wants to keep their defenses up in-house,
To have the enemy imbedded within,
To worry about a friend?

Keep your eyes wide open.
If you sense deception,
Move on!

## Deep in the Well

Let me lower my bucket into your welcoming well:

To dwell deep into the depths;

To unleash the succulent juices of your nature;

To taste the full glory of your essence;

To quench my thirst, my bucket runneth over;

To give me consent;

To come again and again.

# Venom

Your kiss is oh so intoxicating and deadly.
Like the poisonous bite of a black mamba,
You incapacitate me with your venom.

Kissing your breasts is even more lethal.
As your juices drip from my lips,
As blood rushes through my body,
My muscular impulses react.

I am delirious in the moment
As we consummate our love.

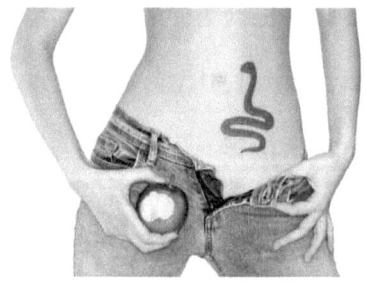

## Touch Me Here

Touch me on my head so I can telepath my feelings for you.

Touch me near my eyes so you can see how deeply I care for you.

Touch me around my lips so I can gently kiss your wrist.

Touch me on my back so you can experience my full embrace.

Touch me on my knees so you can feel me tremble in need.

Touch me in my private place so I can flush my fluids into thee.

But if you touch me on my heart, I will cherish you anew for eternity.

## Love – Where is it?

Love is sought after by many but difficult to find.

It's hard to identify something when you don't know what to look for.

Of course we all have experienced what we thought was love,

But on closer inspection we realized it was something else.

Where do you look? What does it look like? Does it have to be mutual?

When we first catch the scent, our hearts beat faster and we tingle all over,

But this condition could be any number of things.

To accurately identify it do you have to have a certain level of maturity?

Does it have to be rational or make sense?

We often say opposites attract, but does it have staying power?

Does it wane or become stronger the better you know a person?

Does it abide by the same rules for bodily attraction as physics?

In physics gravitational pull causes physical bodies to coalesce and remain intact.

The attraction of love may also remain intact unless a stronger force disrupts it.

Love can also be ephemeral if it is not nurtured.

Oh how complex all the ingredients which determine love and attraction.

True love is a process.

It starts with attraction and slowly builds over time.

It is made up of an unknown mix of brain activity, visuals, values, smells and behaviors.

If it is found it should be cherished and protected with all your heart,

Since once gone, it's difficult to get back and hard to find again.

## Love is Not a Passing Star

Love is not a passing Star,

It is the Sun and the Moon.

It's hot, full of energy, and it lights up your life.

It is friendship on steroids.

It is a natural attraction between heavenly bodies.

Love rotates around a central axis of compatible values, trust, and desire.

It can have high peaks and low valleys but is normally at sea level.

Love combines the super-conscious and subconscious minds in perfect harmony.

It revolves around outside influences but remains steadfast in its commitment.

Love has perturbations and changes with the seasons but remains in orbit.

LOVE is **L**ight, **O**pen, **V**ital, and **E**ndearing.

Transitions

Pursued you
In cyberspace.
Now we've in
Love space.

## Love Is Not Enough

Love is not enough
To sustain a relationship,
To make it through the hard times,
To weather the storm,
To remain committed.

It takes work... lots of it.
It takes a desire to keep the ship afloat,
It takes liking each other,
It takes allowing each other to breathe,
It takes two
To do these things.

## Love Analyzed

Love should not be analyzed,
It should be experienced and enjoyed.
Let it flow within you
And realize
It's potential.

# Falling

As the autumn leaves begin to change their colors and helplessly abandon their summer homes, and the last remaining flowers fight to stay upright, I am reminded of my relationship with you. Our interaction blossomed like the flowers in a field.

Just as the female gamete in the ovule of the flower is fertilized by the male gamete, we consummated our union with a flowering of emotions.

Like the flowers and the trees, we both benefit from this contact. It's a symbiotic relationship where the two are stronger together than separate.

It's like Love.

# Fall

As the leaves begin to fall, I realize how much you remind me of nature in all its illustrious beauty.

A mind like the earth's core with an explosion of exciting thoughts and emotions.

The fiery redness of your flowing locks resembling the late sun and the full moon in all their glory.

How your blue eyes are clear, hypnotizing, and gleaming like the morning sky.

Your lips resemblance to the Hot Lips Plant or a mysterious cave beckoning to be entered.

A neck perfect for kissing standing above shoulders like a gently sloping landscape.

Breasts like the mysterious Twin Peaks Mountain that guards the Virginia Canyon below.

Hips similar to earthen mounds concealing treasures to be desired.

Your feet as you walk on a sun-kissed beach.

As I think about these things I fall in love with you all over again.

# Alley Walking

Looking for love or something else.
Women falling from the sky.
So many little lost sisters.
Decisions, Decisions.
I'll take you...
Ahhh!
♥

## Newness

As the newness of

Our union declines,

Let our love & devotion

Continue to rise.

## Love Transformed

We were madly in love.
We went everywhere together.
We enjoyed each other's company.
We had each other's back.

We never argued.
We thought alike.
You told me you loved me like a brother,
A dear friend.

Should I have caused conflict?
Should I have been a bad boy?
Should I have spent more time with others?
Should I? Should I? Should I?
No.
Maybe we were met to be friends.
Cherish the transformed relationship.

# Amoura

Oh, what a beautiful and sensuous woman,
With your raven hair and cherry lips,
With hips not to be missed.
Let me kiss your neck
And hold your hand,
And let's run away
On a lark.

# Cherries

Life is

A plate of cherries…
May I feast on yours?

Know that one is not enough.
Allow me to continue to eat.

So I will plant the seeds,
To grow more trees,
Of your cherries
For me.

## Don't Tread On Me

They say you are walking all over me.
It's more like driving over me.
I can feel you on my back,
Like you are riding on an asphalt track.

You are undermining my heart's health,
As my brain skids into a wreck,
While having no safety belt,
To save myself from a certain death.

Not anymore I say,
I'm moving on this day,
No matter what you say.

## Truth Be Told

Truth be told,
I'm not that into you anymore.
Not after your cheating stint.
You're not all that, after all.
Your mind is really small.
Let's agree to call it quits,
So I can move all to a better gent.

## Straight from the Heart

I dig you.
I like everything about you.
From the deep recesses of my soul,
My heart throbs for you.

You are within me,
Regulating my pulse,
Controlling my temperature.

With you at my center
I can live on forever,
Or die happy.

# Kiss

Kiss me on my two plump lips,
Insert your tongue real quick.
Slowly caress the tip of mine,
Smile as we synchronize in time.

# Living La Vida Amorosa
(Living the Love Life)

Some are not happy with their life.
I say, love the life you live
And live the life you love.
It's not always easy,
But live it you must.

If you are not doing it now,
A change is in order.
It's all a matter of perspective
And how you view life.
Don't compare your life with others,
They are not you,
They don't have your *je ne sais quoi.*

Focus on the good things about you.
The things that make you special, unique.
If you can accomplish this,
You will be loving life & living the life you love!

## Deep Love

I've known deep love;

The kind of love that reaches deep into your veins and rushes out like an exploding volcano;

The kind of love that strikes a delicate rhythmical balance like the music of a jazz trio: the steady deep pounding of the bass guitar, the excitement of the intricate drum solo, and the virtuoso playing of the piano;

The kind of love that makes your toes curl and then reach for the sky;

The kind of love that sometimes feels like the cold and gives you chills, and other times feels like fireworks and gives you thrills;

The kind of love that makes you laugh and cry at the same time;

The kind of love that makes you feel like you have fallen and can't get up;

The kind of love that beckons you to follow it into the unknown;

The kind of love that compels you to run into a blazing fire to feel the heat;

The kind of love that shakes you up like a 10.0 earthquake on the Modified Mercalli scale.

When you ask yourself, "How Deep is Your Love?" know that it can get really deep!

## Heat

As you enjoy the sun today,
Feel the heat
Of my passion
For you.

## Pleasure

Please give me pleasure now,
Orgasms emanating outward,
Every part of my body tingling.
May we do that again please?

# Marriage

Two people bound together—
Legally, emotionally, spiritually—
Not by ball & chain,
Promised for life.

Will it last?
Some say no.
Does it matter what other's think?

Let's make ours count.
Look deeply into my eyes.
Feel my commitment,
Feel my joy,
Feel my love.

# IV: KEY OF FAMILY

# Family

Who are we?
We are the blood, the light, the glue.
We go back in time and into the future,
A union which cannot be severed,
Bound by our common heritage.
In case you haven't guessed,
We are Family.

## Bad Behavior

Please son,
Don't do that.
It's Not
A good thing to do...
He did it anyway!

# A Family Affair

We are family,
We each have a role,
We support each other,
We are attached by blood,
We are not secret, but open,
We break bread together,
We enjoy each other,
We pray together,
We are children,
We are siblings,
We are parents,
We laugh,
We play,
We love.

# Why Did You Poison Our Son?

You poisoned our son by teaching him to hate and turn against me. You did this by telling him I was mean to him and making up things about me. You rewarded him when he agreed with you. You started this as soon as he could talk, and you continued even after you left.

When he asked you why you didn't take him with you, you lied and told him I wouldn't let you. I didn't have that kind of power, but I was happy to keep him. You didn't want to take him with you, but he was too young to know.

You told people that I didn't help you parent when I did most of it. You told them untruths to make you look good and me bad.

You told people you subsidized me financially when I subsidized you.

Why did you do this? I didn't do anything to you or him to justify your actions.

Even if I did, would it justify poisoning our son and putting him at risk?

Why would you seek to sever the bond between a father and his son, especially since I waited so long to have him?

I told him I loved him.

I was the one who researched to make sure he had the best doctors.

I was the one who had him in my home office most nights helping him with his homework and teaching him about life.

I was the one who researched and took him to all his activities twice during the work week and during weekends.

I was the one to take him to counseling to try to turn his life around.

I was the one who did all the heavy lifting of being a parent.

I taught him to ride a bike.

I even taught you a lot of things but you won't admit that.

The result of your actions was that he started having behavior issues at daycare and at school,

His grades began to suffer,

His anger issues began to increase,

And as was your goal, he begin to hate me: The one he was living with, raising him, and trying to make him successful and to be prepared for life.

He now believes I should not have any say in the matter if he skips school or has bad grades, and that he should not have to obey anything I say.

The problem with poison is that it is not a precise tool like a surgeon's knife. It spreads in all directions and can cause many other debilitating illnesses.

You thought that by poisoning him against me you would be able to control him. It doesn't work that way. You can't control the poison once you administer it.

Now we have a son who exhibits major symptoms of poisoning late in his high school years: Behavior issues, loss of motivation, skipping school, drugs, and hate.

Unfortunately, he will realize when he leaves high school that the world won't care about his success as much as I do:

His employer will not tolerate him not showing up or being late for work,

The people he thought were his friends could turn out to be his worst enemies,

He will realize it's more expensive to live than he thought,

He will realize that life is tough when you must fend for yourself.

But not to worry, he won't blame you, he will blame me.

We can only hope at this point that a cure for his poison can be found.

## Raising Children

Caged birds can't get out.
It's not safe for them to be out,
But they don't know that yet.
Will they understand
Once they are allowed to fly?
The jury is still out.

# Family Tree

As I browse through my family tree
I see many hidden faces,
Covering the days of old,
When slavery was in vogue.

Who were those cotton pickers?
Field Hands?
Servants?
How did they live?
How did they die?

Somehow many survived,
Though they had miserable lives;
But some went on to be
Part of my family tree.

## Siblings

It's good to have siblings.
Unlike an only child,
You have people to play with,
To talk too,
To play mischief on your parents with.
Sure you have to learn to share,
To get along,
To compete for attention,
But that's what life is about:
Being prepared to deal with the real world,
To give, to compete, to survive.

## You Can Always Go Back Home

Heading out on your own and leaving home,
To see the world and to show you are grown.
A leap of faith into the unknown,
To make your mark before you are gone.

It may sound scary but fear not.
Take care of yourself and do your best.
You have to take your shot
So make the most of it.

If things get tough
Show your mettle
And try not to settle,
But also know when to fold.

Success or failure though,
It's always good to know
That you can always go back home.

# V: KEY OF INTERACTION WITH NATURE

# Weeds

Weeds in your garden.

You spent long days

In the sun.

Just smell

The roses.

# Spring

The drabness and cold of winter has succumb
to the freshness and warmth of spring.
Flowers, flowers everywhere.
Smell the lilac, the lavender, the jasmine:
Reds, whites, purples dazzle the eye.

Oh how glorious it is.
A feast to the senses.
Enjoy it now
Before it is gone.

## Phases

Phases exist
In one plane,
Transcend to
New dimensions,
Here we are again.

# The Wind

I love the summer wind
As it blazes through the sky,
Dancing its Irish jig,
Singing it's songs of joy.

It feels so good on my skin
While serenading me again and again.
But don't let it get too excited,
Because a tornado could begin,
And then it's no longer my friend.

## Ocean Waves

Sky blue ocean waves
Meandering down the shore,
Shifting through the sand
As they crash into the land.

# Black Bird

Black bird in the sky above
Singing songs of love,
Glistening in the sun,
Basking in its glory.

Oh, how I wish I was one,
To reach for the stars at night,
Incognito in flight,
Until caught by the moon light!

# VI: KEY OF MIND STREAMS

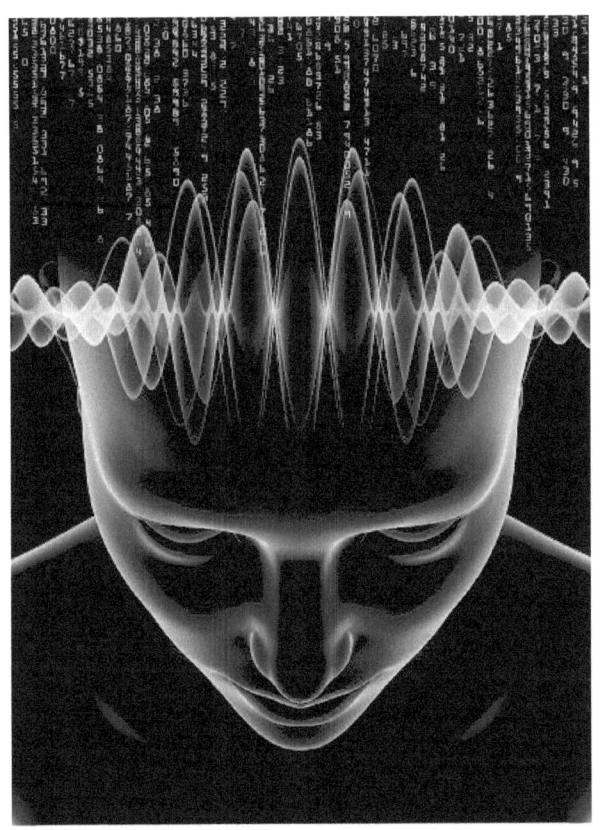

## Knowledge

Men in search
Of knowledge
Will never
Be lost.

## Questions

Looking for answers,
Who has the answers?
What are the questions?
Not sure I know.
All I know is
That I am confused.

?

## Popsicle Stick

You call me a Popsicle stick
Because of my skinny frame and red lips,
But anorexia is no joke.
You should be helping me to cope,
Instead you are acting like a dope.

This is a mental illness
And I have feelings.
It not only impacts me,
But also my dear family.

You will not lick me!
I will ignore your goading
And put my recovery in motion,
By seeking the right treatment,
So my family and I can survive and thrive.

## Black and White

### Past

Growing up in the South, separate but equal.

Not so equal, don't understand.

"For whites only" water fountains.

Laws designed to discriminate.

Whites with pools, preventive care, Suburbs.

Blacks with ditches, emergency care, Projects.

Black-white relationships taboo, illegal.

White majority treating minorities horribly.

Wasn't this country created because of injustice elsewhere?

### Present

Integrated but separate.

Equal laws, unequal implementation, progress.

Better access to services, facilities and public accommodations.

May need more money or better job.

Minority advancements, black president, positive role models, white concern.

Black-white relationships more common, white women 'stealing' black men.

Smaller white majority.

Shouldn't we be united against more dangerous issues?

### Future

Minorities the new majority.

Some refusing to accept the new reality.

Can now concentrate on more pressing issues:

Hunger, poverty, violence and terrorism, health issues, inequality, climate change, habitat and biodiversity loss, pollution.

Everything is Grey.

Have we wasted too much time?

## Trading Places

We exchange ourselves:
You are me, I am you.
No one knows but us.
Not very comfortable.
Let's Not.

## Way

Just because
You can't see a way
Doesn't mean that
There isn't a way.

It's out there.
It just has to be found.
Don't be discouraged,
Stay focused to find the solution.

## Bias in Our Midst

There is bias in our midst.
Bigotry waves are adrift,
Invading our peaceful existence.
Marvin Gaye asked "What's Going On?"
We know what's going on.
We just can't stop it.
We don't want to admit it.

What will it take,
To change the pace,
To eliminate
This national disgrace?

# Energize

On a warm summer day
When the days are long,
The sun is high,
And all living things
Seem to slow down,
Utilize the heat
To energize your body
And soul,
To power your way
Back to life.

# Coming Out

So you are hidden or undercover,
Religious, non-religious,
Political, apolitical,
Introverted,
Afraid,
Gay.

It's time to come out.
Like a stunning flower
In full bloom,
You are an important part
Of the human landscape.

Don't be afraid.
Move front and center.
Like a peacock strutting down a runway,
Spread your wings
And set yourself free.

# Majority

You can't allow
The Majority
To define
The Minority.

# Tommie Smith

Tommie Smith, punished during the 1968 Mexico Olympics for raising his fist.

He and John Carlos peacefully protesting injustices as was their right.

But he would not flee, even though they would not let him be;

Attempting to keep him from finding work and denying his worth.

But Oberlin College would not bite as they set him in their sights.

Offering him a job as a track coach, not out of spite, but because it was right.

He was my track coach, so I had insight into his might;

Watching him run like a gazelle in flight.

Oberlin's motto is "*Learning* and *Labor*."

By hiring Tommie, we *learned* peaceful protest was the right move.

For those who *labored* under his tutorage, it was the right groove.

His presence was inspirational and being on his team was sensational.

Tommie took a fist and Colin took a knee.

They took his metal and took Colin's helmet.

I am still waiting to see in 2019,

The day when equality allows all us to be free.

## Waves

If there are big waves

In your life,

Just think

You are at the beach!

## Lost

Looking for meaning in life.

One theme is all I need

So that I can say with esteem,

That I accomplished my dream.

## Wanderer

I am a wanderer;
A mind-mover shifting through space,
Looking here and there,
Trying to understand:
Contemplating,
Observing,
Visualizing,
Slicing through the universe
To connect the dots,
To bring meaning
To this place in which we live.

# The God within Us

We are all God,
In a spiritual way,
Infinitely connected as one.
Our spirit never dies,
But changes in form.
We all sit on the throne of humanity,
With the capability for universal love.

We also have competing forces
Attempting to lead us astray,
Don't let that happen,
Don't be deceived.
Harness your power against the intruder,
So your internal truth can rule supreme.

# VII: KEY OF RETIREMENT & DEATH

# Retirement

Hump day has arrived.
Enjoying my morning coffee
While watching birds and butterflies;
Slight breeze tickling my ears
Like the soft tunes of a jazz pianist.
As cars pull out of their driveways
The realization hits…
I don't have to go anywhere!

## Joy Delayed

I dreamed of what I would do in retirement:
To catch up on my reading,
To travel the world,
To enjoy my wife's company,
To sleep in!

But then life happened:
Financial difficulty,
Poor health,
Wife left.
Don't wait.
Do it now!

## Closed Door

Behind the closed door,
An unknown culmination of life.
Is it darkness or light?
I do not want to enter,
But I must.
Wish me luck.

# Black Hole

Being pulled against my will,
My body withering like a mature orchid,
Longing to find meaning,
Purpose:
Why was I here?
Why am I leaving?
Dimming light...
Darkness.

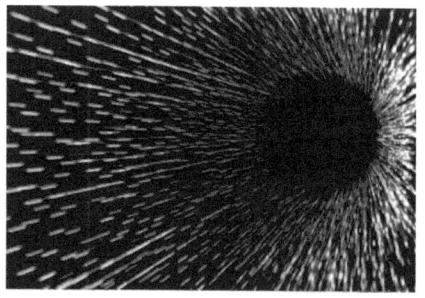

## Mourning

Missing you already.

Our time together was too short.

Until we are able to meet again,

Running in the heavens,

Napping on the clouds,

I will continue with this life,

Needing to imagine

Growing old together.

# REBIRTH

Life is an illusion.

Energy can never be created nor destroyed.

So may be the case for mankind.

Death is the beginning of a rebirth, an awakening to a new life, soul, being.

Let's not waste it this time.

Be frugal, charitable, open, accepting, and loving.

The universe is big enough for all us in some form, state, existence.

Share it and respect it, and we shall all live on in peace and harmony.

# ABOUT THE AUTHOR

Henry Lee Thomas was born in Columbus, Georgia but has lived in many regions of the United States and has traveled throughout the world. He is a middle child from a large family and he has an unending thirst for knowledge.

He has a B.A. in Mathematics from Oberlin College in Oberlin, OH and an M.S. in Operations Research from the University of Iowa in Iowa City, IA.

His diverse background, along with his introspective way of thinking allows him to see poetry from a unique perspective.

His other book dealt with being a single parent:

Men's Guide to Being a Single Parent: Different Animal than Women Single Parents
ISBN-13: 978-0615990668
ISBN-10: 0615990665

www.ingramcontent.com/pod-product-compliance
Lightning Source LLC
Chambersburg PA
CBHW060532080526
44586CB00012B/711